Grimm's Fairytales on Stage

A collection of plays based on the Brothers Grimm's fairytales

By
Julie Meighan

First published in 2020
by
JemBooks
Cork,
Ireland
dramastartbooks.com

ISBN: 978-9163195-2-3

All rights reserved.

No part of this book may be reproduced or utilised in any form or by any electronic, digital or mechanical means, including information storage, photocopying, filming, recording, video recording and retrieval systems, without prior permission in writing from the publisher. The only exception is by a reviewer, who may quote short excerpts in a review. The moral rights of the author have been asserted.

Text Copyright © 2020, Julie Meighan

About the Author

Julie Meighan is a lecturer in Drama in Education at the Cork Institute of Technology. She has taught drama to all age groups and levels. She is the author of the Amazon bestselling *Drama Start: Drama Activities, Plays and Monologues for Young Children (Ages 3 -8)* ISBN 978-0956896605, *Drama Start Two: Drama Activities and Plays for Children (Ages 9-12)* ISBN 978-0-9568966-1-2 and *Stage Start: 20 Plays for Children (Ages 3-12)* ISBN 978-0956896629.

Contents

The Elves and the Shoemaker..1

The Musicians of Bremen..4

Hansel and Gretel..8

Rumpelstiltskin..13

Snow White & the Seven Dwarfs..19

The Cat and the Mouse...25

The Frog Prince...28

Little Red Riding Hood...32

The Pied Piper of Hamelin..36

The Elves and the Shoemaker

Characters: Shoemaker, his wife, three customers, three narrators, and four elves.

Narrator 1: There once lived a shoemaker who was very kind but very poor.

Narrator 2: He and his wife had nothing to eat. *(The Shoemaker and his wife are centre stage; the shoemaker is looking at some leather he has and the wife is looking around the kitchen for some food.)*

Shoemaker: I'm so hungry! I have only got this one piece of leather left. *(He holds ups the leather.)* I will leave it here and make the shoes in the morning.

Wife: Let's go to bed. *(They go to the side of the stage and go to sleep.)*

Narrator 3: The next morning, the shoemaker woke up and came downstairs.

Narrator 1: On his table were the most beautiful shoes he had ever seen.

Shoemaker: *(Looks admiringly at the shoes.)* Am I dreaming?

Wife: *(Shocked.)* Who made these marvellous shoes?

(A customer walks into the shop, so they stop talking, smile and greet her.)

Customer 1: Oh my, what beautiful shoes! I must have them. Here, keep the change. *(She gives the shoemaker money and exits the shop.)*

Shoemaker: Look, we have enough money to buy leather for two pairs of shoes and some food. *(The shoemaker and his wife hug each other and jump up and down with excitement.)*

Narrator 2: The next day, the shoemaker and his wife woke up and found two pairs of shoes. They were more beautiful than the first pair.

Wife: Oh, what beautiful shoes. Who is making them?

Shoemaker: I don't know.

Customer 2: *(Enters.)* I just saw those shoes in the window. Can I buy them?

Shoemaker: Certainly. *(Gives her the shoes.)*

Customer 2: Keep the change. *(Exits the shop.)*

(Customer 3 enters, very excited.)

Customer 3: I just saw the most beautiful shoes in the window. Can I buy them?

Shoemaker: Certainly. *(Gives her the second pair of shoes.)*

Customer 3: Keep the change. *(Exits the shop.)*

Shoemaker: *(Looks at money.)* Now I've enough money to buy four pieces of leather.

Narrator 3: Over the next few weeks, the shoe shop became very popular.

Narrator 1: The shoemaker and his wife went to bed every night.

Narrator 2: And every morning, there were always new shoes waiting to be sold.

Shoemaker: I can't work it out. What kind of magic is making all these beautiful shoes? I've a plan. *(He whispers to his wife. Both of them whisper to each other. The audience can't hear.)*

Narrator 3: So that night, instead of going to bed like they usually did, they hid behind the table.

Narrator 1: When the clock struck midnight, four elves came in tiptoeing into the room.

Elf 1: Look, he has left more leather.

Elf 2: Let's make some shoes for the kind old man and his wife.

Elf 3: They will be so happy when they see these beautiful shoes.

Elf 4: Come, it's time to leave; be quiet everyone. (*They tiptoe quietly and slowly and exit the stage. Shoemaker and his wife come out from behind the table.*)

Wife: They have made us rich.

Shoemaker: We have to return the favour, and I've a plan. (*He whispers in his wife's ear and she nods her head.*)

Narrator 1: So the old man and his wife worked all day to make the elves little green suits and shoes.

Narrator 2: When the clock struck midnight, the shoemaker and his wife hid behind the table again and waited. (*The elves tiptoe in the room very quietly.*)

Elf 1: Sssshhh!

Elf 2: Look at these. (*Holds up the elves' suits and shoes.*)

Elf 3: This is the most beautiful present anyone has ever given us.

Elf 4: Let's put them on. (*They admire themselves and jump up and down with excitement.*)

Narrator 3: The old man and his wife never saw the elves again.

Narrator 1: But they never went hungry again because they were so rich from selling shoes that they never had to work again.

The Musicians of Bremen

Characters: Three storytellers, Farmer, Farmer's Wife, Donkey, Dog, Cat, Rooster, four robbers.

Storyteller 1: Once upon a time there lived a farmer and his wife.

Storyteller 2: They were very cruel to all the animals on the farmer.

Farmer: *(kicks the dog)* Dog you are so LAZY. Get to work at once.

Farmer's Wife: Cat, stop sleeping. Go chase some mice.

Farmer: Look, at that Donkey. He is ready for the Knackers yard.

Farmer' wife: He is too old to do any challenging work. We should get rid of him.

Farmer: What's for dinner?

Farmer's Wife: I'm going to make rooster stew. Your favourite.

(The rooster overhears the conversation. He is very upset. Farmer and Farmer' wife exit.)

Storyteller 3: The rooster jumped on top of the chicken coop and began to crow as loud as he could. All the animals were very confused.

Cat: What's going on?

Dog: It's morning already. I forgot to go to sleep.

Donkey: Don't be silly. The sun has only dipped below the horizon. Something very strange is happening.

Cat: Rooster, why are you crowing at this time of day?

Rooster: I thought I should crow one last time because the farmer's Wife is going to put me in the cooking pot for tonight's dinner.

Storyteller 1: All the animals were horrified.

Dog: The farmer and his wife are so mean to us poor animals.

Cat: They work us so hard, and they never allow us to rest.

Donkey: I've an idea that might save the rooster.

Rooster: Well, I'm all ears. What's your plan?

Donkey: Let's run away to Bremen and join the town musicians.

Rooster: Excellent plan. Let's pack our bags and go straight away.

Storyteller 2: That evening, the cat, the dog, the donkey and the rooster crept out of the farmyard and set off on the road to Bremen.

Storyteller 3: They walked through the woods in the dead of night. The animals began to get cold and hungry.

Dog: I'm so cold. *(He starts shivering.)*

Cat: I see a light over there. It's coming from a little cottage over there.

Donkey: Let's knock on the door, the owners may let us rest there for the night.

Dog: They may even give us some food.

Storyteller 1: All the animals peer into the window of the house.

Storyteller 2: They saw a massive table which had an array of delicious food on it. *(Four robbers come in with sacks of money.)*

Robber 1: That was a goodnight's work.

Robber 2: *(spreads the money out on the table.)* Now, it's time to count our money.

Robber 3: I'm hungry. I want to eat this delicious food.

Robber 4: Robbing banks does make you hungry. *(All the robbers go to the table and start eating the food.)*

Cat: If only inside the cottage by the fire, eating that lovely food.

Donkey: I've another plan. *(All the animals huddled together.)* Dog, stand on top of me.

Dog: Cat, stand on top of me.

Cat: Rooster, stand on top of me.

Donkey: Are we ready? One, two, three, sing. *(The donkey brays, the dog barks, the cat meows. The rooster crows.)*

Robber 1: What's that noise.

Robber 2: HELP! We are being attacked.

Robber 3: by a singing, four-headed monster.

Robber 4: Run, run, save yourself. *(The robbers run as fast as they can out of the cottage.)*

Rooster: Everyone tuck into the delicious food. *(All the animals race to the table and eat the food and then sit by the warm fire. Robbers on the side of the stage. They are all shivering.)*

Robber 1: I'm cold and hungry.

Robber 2: We should go back.

Robber 3: Off you go then.

Robber 4: I'm staying here. I never want to see that singing monster again.

Storyteller 1: One of the robbers crept back into the house. Everything was in darkness. He lit a match and startled the cat who flew at him. *(Cat jumps up. He spits and scratches the robber.)*

Storyteller 2: Then, the robber tripped over the dog who got a fright and bit him.

Storyteller 3: The donkey woke up and kicked the robber with his hind legs.

Storyteller 1: The rooster was women out of his slumber and started to crow. The robber got such a fright he ran back to his friends in the wood.

Robber 3: What happened?

Robber 4: You look like you have seen a ghost.

Robber 2: You aren't going to believe what happened.

Robber 1: Tell us.

Robber 2: Well, first, an evil witch spat and scratched me. Then I was stabbed by a savage beast, and then a two-headed monster beat me with a stick and then a vile vampire screamed at me to leave.

Storyteller 1: The robbers left the woods for good and never returned. The animals had all the food and money they could wish for.

Storyteller 2: They lived a life of luxury.

Storyteller 3: They never did make it to Bremen.

Hansel and Gretel

Characters: Three storytellers, Hansel, Gretel, Stepmother, Father, Blackbird, Old Witch.

Storyteller 1: Once upon a time, long, long agar.

Storyteller 2: There lived a boy called Hansel.

Storyteller 3: Hansel had a sister called Gretel whom he loved very much, they lived with their father and their mean, nasty stepmother.

(The children are playing, laughing and having fun.)

Stepmother: Dinner time.

Hansel: At last I'm so hungry.

Gretel: Me too.

(They run into the house and sit at the table.)

Hansel: *(whispers to Gretel)* Is this supposed to be dinner? It is only a slice of bread.

Gretel: Sssshhh just eat it. Don't let stepmother hear you. You will make her angry.

Hansel: *(louder)* but I'm starving.

Stepmother: Stop complaining. We have no money. Bread is all we can afford.

(Father enters and the stepmother looks at him in disgust.)

Why did I have to marry a poor woodcutter?

Father: I'm sorry children that there's no more food but times are hard. People have new gas fires, and nobody wants to buy wood anymore.

Hansel: It is alright, father. I quite like stale bread. *(He makes a face as she is trying to chew it.)*

Gretel: Yummy.

(They look at each other and make faces while they eat.)

Stepmother: Time for bed children.

Children: Good night. *(Hansel and Gretel leave the stage.)*

Stepmother: *(angrily)* Why did I have to marry a worthless man like you. And to make matters worse, you have two pesky children who are always starving.

Woodcutter: I'm sorry. I'm trying my best to put food on the table.

Stepmother: Well, there is nothing for it. The children must go.

Father: What? I can't get rid of my children. I love them too much.

Stepmother: Unless you can come up with a better solution, they must go.

Woodcutter: Please don't take my children.

Stepmother: That's settled tomorrow we take them deep in the woods and leave them there.

(Hansel and Gretel come back on stage. They heard the conversation and Gretel starts to cry.)

Hansel: Don't worry Gretel, I have an idea.

Storyteller 1: The next day....

Stepmother: Wake up, my darlings. It's such a lovely day. We are all going to go for a walk in the woods. Here, take some bread in case you get hungry.

Gretel: Hansel, I'm scared.

Hansel: We will find our way back, I promise.

(*Hansel starts to leave bread crumbs behind him as he walks.*)

Stepmother: We should rest here, children. I'm just off to collect some wood for a fire. Ear the bread I gave you for lunch.

Stepmother: Ha, ha. They will never find their way back.

Storyteller 2: They waited for hours, and the stepmother never came back.

Storyteller 3: Soon, they huddled together and fell asleep.

Hansel: (*suddenly wakes up*) Wake up, Gretel. I'm cold, and it's dark. Let's find our bread trail, and we will make our way home.

Gretel: Shoo, shoo, the birds have eaten out bread trail.

Hansel: It's gone.

Gretel: What will we do now?

Hansel: Let's just walk until we find our way out of the woods.

Storyteller 1: They walked all day, and that night they fell asleep, huddled tightly together to keep warm.

Storyteller 2: They were tired and hungry. The next day, they woke up and continued their journey.

Storyteller 3: Soon, they came to a clearing in the wood, and they saw a little house.

Hansel: Let's call and see if anyone is home.

Gretel: They may give us some food.

Storyteller 1: As they walked closer to the house, they noticed something very unusual about the house.

Hansel: (*amazed*) the house is made of gingerbread.

Gretel: It looks delicious.

Hansel: Let's eat some. I'm sure the owner won't mind.

Storyteller 2: They started to eat the house when the door flew opened, and out popped a little old witch.

Storyteller 2: She was very ugly and bent over.

Witch: Enjoying my house, are you?

Hansel: Yes, it is scrumptious.

Witch: Oh, do come inside. I don't get many visitors.

Gretel: What a kind old woman.

(The old woman gave them lots of food, sweets, chocolates, cakes.)

Witch: Please stay the night and make an old woman happy. I don't get many visitors.

Hansel and Gretel: We would love to stay here.

Storyteller 3: The next morning, Gretel woke up. She couldn't find Hansel.

Gretel: Hansel, Hansel. Where are you?

Witch: Good morning, dear. You are just in time to help me cook lunch.

Gretel: Have you seen Hansel? I can't find him.

Witch: Don't worry about him, dear. He is just fine. Take this tray of food outside to him.

(The witch gives Gretel the tray and she takes it but looks confused when she sees Hansel locked in a cage.)

Gretel: Hansel, what are doing locked in a cage? *(She tries to open it.)*

Hansel: The kind old woman is really a wicked old witch. She has locked me in the cage so she can fatten me up and eat me.

Gretel: Hansel, I'll get you out I'd here. Don't worry, I've a plan.

(Witch enters.)

Witch: Hold out your finger. You are so thin. You need to eat more.

Storyteller 1: The witch kept Hansel in the cage and treated Gretel like a servant. One day the witch.

Witch: Today is the day, I'm going to eat Hansel. I think at last he is fat enough. I must get the oven ready.

Storyteller 1: The witch bent over the oven, and Gretel took the opportunity to push her in.

Storyteller 2: She slammed the door shut.

Gretel: Good riddance, old witch.

Witch: I'm melting.

(Gretel runs to the cage and opens it. Hansel and Gretel hug.)

Hansel: Thank you for saving me, Gretel.

Gretel: The witch is gone forever.

Hansel: Look at all those jewels, money and gold.

Blackbird: I'm sorry I ate your bread trail. I can take you home, just follow me.

(They reached home and the woodcutter was so happy to see them.)

Father: I'm so happy you are back. I got rid of your evil stepmother. She won't bother us again.

Rumpelstiltskin

Characters: Three storytellers, Miller, Baker, Butcher, Candlestick maker, Miller's Daughter/Queen, Old Man/Rumpelstiltskin, King, Guard, Subjects.

Storyteller 1: Once upon a time, there lived a miller, he had a beautiful daughter. One day he said.

Miller: It's about time I found a suitable suitor for my daughter to marry.

Storyteller 2: Word got around the village that the miller was looking for a husband for his beautiful daughter.

Storyteller 3: Soon, the butcher arrived with a large box of delicious meat.

Butcher: May I have your daughter's hand in marriage?

Miller: She is the most beautiful girl in all the land. She is far too good for you. She can spin straw into gold.

Storyteller 3: Then, the baker arrived with a large box of delicious cakes, bread and pies.

Baker: May I have your daughter's hand in marriage?

Miller: She is the most beautiful girl in all the land. She is far too good for you. She can spin straw into gold.

Storyteller 3: After a while, the candlestick maker arrived with a large box of scented candles.

Candlestick maker: May I have your daughter's hand in marriage?

Miller: She is the most beautiful girl in all the land. She is far too good for you. She can spin straw into gold.

Storyteller 1: Word reached the king of the miller's daughters talents.

King: This is incredible. I've never heard talent like this before. A girl that can spin straw into gold. Guard, bring the miller's daughter to me at once. *(The guard goes off stage and gets the millers daughter. She bows before him.)*

King: I hear you spin straw into gold.

Miller's Daughter: Well, I can spin straw but not....

King: Excellent. I'm going to lock you into this room with straw and a spinning wheel. You will turn every bit of it into gold.

Miller's Daughter: But, Your Majesty. You don't understand.

King: Silence, if you fail to turn this straw into gold, your father will be punished severely. Guard, lock her in.

Guard: Start spinning.

Miller's Daughter: How could my father have told such lies. I've no idea how to spin straw into

gold. What shall I do? *(She starts to cry.)*

Storyteller 1: Then, out of nowhere, a small man with pointed ears appears.

Small Man: Why are you crying?

Miller's Daughter: *(startled)* I've to spin all this straw into gold by morning; otherwise, my father will be punished.

Old Man: I can do it for you. But you must give me something in return.

Miller's Daughter: Here, take my locket.

Old Man: Thanks.

Storyteller 2: The old man got to work, and the miller's Daughter fell fast asleep,

Storyteller 3: The next morning, when the miller's Daughter woke up, the man had vanished, and the room was filled with gold. *(The door opens and the guard walks in, followed by the king. The miller's Daughter bows.)*

King: How wonderful, you did it. All the straw has been turned to gold.

Storyteller 1: The king took her to a bigger room which was filled with straw.

King: Start spinning. I'll return in the morning all the straw must be turned to gold.

Miller's Daughter: Little old man, where are you?

Old man: I'm here. I'll spin the straw into gold. What will you give me in return?

Miller's Daughter: Here take my ring. It is my most precious possession.

Old Man: Thanks.

Storyteller 2: The old man goes to work, and the miller's Daughter fell fast asleep,

Storyteller 3: The next morning, when the miller's Daughter woke up, the man had vanished, and the room was filled with gold. *(The door opens and the guard walks in, followed by the king. The miller's Daughter bows.)*

King: How wonderful, you did it. All the straw has been turned to gold.

Storyteller 1: The king took her to a bigger room which was filled with straw.

King: Start spinning. I'll return in the morning all the straw must be turned to gold.

Miller's Daughter: Little old man, where are you?

Old man: I'm here. I'll spin the straw into gold. What will you give me in return?

Miller's Daughter: I've nothing else to give you.

Old Man: Oh, yes, you do. When the king marries you, and you become queen, then you must give me your first-born child.

Miller's Daughter: I'm so tired. I can't be bothered arguing. Anyway, the king won't keep his promise.

Storyteller 1: The old man worked through the night. The miller's Daughter slept, and in the morning, the king flung open the door.

King: What wondrous wealth. Wake up, girl.

(The girl wakes up, she stretches and yawns.)

King: I have never noticed how beautiful you are. Please forgive me, I've been so greedy. *(He gets down on one knee.)* If you agree to be my queen, I will never make you spin straw into gold.

Miller's Daughter: I would love to be your queen.

Storyteller 1: They got married the next day, and soon the queen had a beautiful baby boy.

Storyteller 2: One night, while the queen was putting the baby to bed. Out from nowhere, the little old man appeared.

Miller's Daughter: You startled me. What do you want?

Old man: I've come to take what is rightfully mine. *(Old man tries to grab the baby, but the miller's Daughter holds on tightly.)*

Miller's Daughter: Please don't take my baby. I'll give you anything else you desire.

Old Man: Your majesty, *(he bows)* do you forget that I can spin all the gold I desire. You promised me your first-born child. *(He takes the baby.)*

Miller's Daughter: *(starts crying)* please don't take him. I'll do anything you ask.

Old Man: Well, if you can guess at the end of three days I'll let you keep your child, if not he will be mine forever. *(Old man laughs wickedly, hands back the baby and disappears.)*

Storyteller 3: The queen sat down and listed as many names as she could think of.

Miller's Daughter: Balthazar, Funny face, Bandy-legs, Oh, it is no good I'll have to travel around the kingdom and collect as many names as I can.

Storyteller 1: The next day, the queen hopped on her horse and travelled the length and breadth of the kingdom, collecting unusual names. *(Queen mimes speaking to villagers, collecting names and writing them down. This can be a movement sequence, and music can be played for effect.)*

Miller's Daughter/Queen: Oh dear, I'll never get it right. *(she sees smoke rising from a tree in the woods.)* What's, is that over there?

Storyteller 2: The queen walked towards the smoke, and she couldn't believe her eyes or her luck.

Storyteller 3: She saw the old man leaping around the fire singing

Rumpelstiltskin: The queen will never win this game because Rumpelstiltskin is my name.

Queen: Yes! Result! Now I have him.

Storyteller 1: On the third day at midnight, the old man once again visited the queen.

Old Man: Queen, what is my name?

Miller's Daughter/Queen: Why that is easy. Rumpelstiltskin is your name.

Old Man: Drat! How did you know?

Miller's Daughter/Queen: You always looked like a Rumpelstiltskin to me. *(He stamped his feet so hard that the ground cracked under him and he disappeared.)*

Miller's Daughter/Queen: *(waves down the hole)* Bye, bye. Good riddance.

All Storytellers: Rumpelstiltskin was never seen again.

Snow White & the Seven Dwarfs

Characters: Narrator, Wicked Queen, Snow White, Seven Dwarfs, Huntsman, Handsome Prince, Mirror.

(Curtains open with Snow White on one side of the stage, sitting down reading a book and the Queen on the other side of the stage looking at Snow White angrily)

Narrator: Once upon a time, in a land far, far away, lived a beautiful young Princess. She had hair as dark as night and skin as white as snow, and so, she was called Snow White. She was kind and gentle, and people would stop and stare at her beauty. Snow White lived in a beautiful castle with her father, the King. One day, her father remarried. Although the new Queen was very beautiful, she was cruel and unkind. The new Queen did not like Snow White and was very jealous of her because she was so beautiful. *(Snow White skips off the stage and the Queen stays on stage. The Mirror is carried on)*

Queen: Aw, at last, my mirror has arrived. *(The queen admires herself in the mirror.)* Mirror, mirror on the wall, who is the fairest of them all?

Mirror: My dear Queen, you are indeed very beautiful, but it is Snow White, who is the fairest of them of all.

Queen: *(outraged)* What? This cannot be. I shall have her killed and then I will be the fairest in the land... Huntsman, come here at once!

Huntsman: *(stammers)* Y-y-yes, Your Majesty?

Queen: I order you to take Snow White into the woods immediately, and kill her. Now go!! Get out of my sight! (*The Queen walks off stage stamping her feet angrily and the Huntsman stands to the front of the stage.*)

Huntsman: What shall I do? I don't want to kill Snow White, she is so good and kind. But the Queen will be so angry if I do not do what she says. Oh no!(*The Huntsman walks off the stage looking sad. The background changes to a woods scene, and Snow White and the Huntsman enter onto the stage.*)

Snow White: Where are we going?

Huntsman: We must go into the woods. I am so very sorry; the Queen has ordered me to kill you, but I cannot do it. You must run away and never return, or we will both be killed. Run, quickly! (*Snow White runs off the stage.*)

Huntsman: What shall I do now? Lie to the Queen? Perhaps she will believe me... (*Huntsman runs off stage.*)

Narrator: The Huntsman returned to the Castle and told the Queen that he had killed Snow White.

Huntsman: Snow White is dead, Your Majesty. (*He bows.*)

Queen: Very good! Very good, Snow White is gone. Now go! Mirror, mirror on the wall, who is the fairest of them all? (*Huntsman runs off stage*)

Mirror: My dear Queen, I must inform you that Snow White is still alive... and she is the fairest of them all.

Queen: The Huntsman lied to me! I see that if I want this done, I shall do it myself... I shall find Snow White and kill her (*Evil laugh!*)

Narrator: Meanwhile, Snow White was lost and alone in the woods but could not return to the castle. She sat down on the ground and began to cry.

Narrator: Snow White carried on walking into the woods until she came to a little house. She knocked on the door (*she knocks*) but no one answered, so she went inside. She found herself in a small kitchen with a little table surrounded by seven little chairs; in the bedroom, she found seven little beds.

Snow White: How very strange. I wonder who lives here. Whoever they are, they are very messy. This house is filthy! It will take me all day to get this place cleaned up, I'd better get started. (*Snow White starts cleaning.*)

Snow White: There! All done! (*yawns*) I'm so tired, I think I'll just have a little nap. (*The seven dwarfs return after a hard day of work.*)

Grumpy: The door is wide open!

Doc: I think we need to fix the lock on that door.

Sleepy: I'm tired! (*rubbing eyes.*) Can I go to bed now? (*Yawns and stretches.*)

Sneezy: Achoo!! (*Blows his nose really loudly on a handkerchief.*)

Dopey: Huh, what's going on?

Happy: Wow, look at this place! It's so clean... Who did this?

Bashful: Hey, look! I think we have a visitor. Look at her! She's so pretty! (*Looks away shyly*)

(*The dwarfs surround the sleeping Snow White. She wakes up suddenly with a fright and looks around*)

Snow White: Who are you?

Grumpy: You're the one in our house. Who are you?

Snow White: I'm Snow White, and I have nowhere else to go. Please can I stay here for just a little while? Please? I can be very helpful; I can clean, and sew, and cook...

Happy: You can cook? Great, you can stay! I'm famished. What's for dinner? I'm Happy by the way.

Doc: I'm Doc.

Dopey: I'm Dopey.

Bashful: I'm Bashful.

Sneezy: I-I-I'm Sneezy, achoo!!

Sleepy: (*Yawning and stretching*) I'm Sleepy!

Grumpy: Hold on one second here! I don't like this, not one bit. She's not staying, and that's final.

Doc: Don't mind him, that's Grumpy!!

Dopey: I'm starving. Can we eat now, please?

(*The other dwarfs ignore Grumpy's complaints and he stands with his arms folded in a huff, while the other dwarfs sit at the table*)

Snow White: There you go! Eat up! (*Snow white serves each dwarf some food.*)

Doc: Mmmmm, delicious!

(*Grumpy smells the food and slowly walks over and sits down at the table, still looking angry, and starts eating.*)

Narrator: So, Snow White stayed with the dwarfs, who were very happy to have a girl around at last. Even Grumpy didn't mind it so much once he'd tasted Snow White's cooking. They were all very happy living together. The dwarfs soon began caring about Snow White very much. They went off to work each morning, and Snow White took very good care of their little house.

(*Snow White goes back to her cleaning. Then there's a knock at the door.*)

Snow White: Oh, I wonder who that could be.

(*In walks the Queen, dressed as an old woman.*)

Snow White: Oh hello, would you like to come in?

Old woman: Hello dear! I was just walking in the woods when I saw you being so busy cleaning. You must be very tired. Would you like one of my delicious red apples? They are very, very tasty!

Snow White: Oh, they do look very delicious, and I am a little peckish. Oh dear, I'm not sure if I should. My father always told me to never take food from a stranger! Then again, he also told me to get married before I moved in with a man, and here I am, living with seven... What should I do? Should I take the apple?

Old Woman: Go on, dear, it's only an apple!! (*Laughs to herself*)

Snow White: Alright, then. Maybe just one little bite. It can't hurt...

(*Snow White takes a bite and collapses to the ground. The Old Woman throws off her disguise and laughs evilly*)

Queen: Hahaha!! My plan has worked, Snow White has eaten the poisonous apple, and now she is gone, gone, gone! I shall be the fairest in the land at last. Hahahaha!!

(*The Queen runs off the stage.*)

(*A little while later the dwarfs walk on stage - "I Ho, I Ho" plays - and find Snow White unconscious.*)

Happy: Oh no, what happened? Is she dead?

Doc: (*Holding up the apple and smelling it.*) No, she's not dead, but she has been poisoned.

Grumpy: It wasn't me!

(*The dwarfs get down on their knees and surround Snow White. They all begin to cry.*)

Sleepy: She is too beautiful to bury.

Sneezy: We can't place her in the cold ground.

Bashful: I have a plan. Let's place her in a glass coffin.

Narrator: The dwarfs placed Snow White in a glass coffin. They visited her every day and brought her flowers. A year and a day later, a handsome prince came riding by. *(He gets off his horse.)*

Handsome Prince: I've never seen such a beautiful girl! *(He bends down and kisses her. Snow White wakes up.)*

Snow White: What happened? Where am I?

Dwarfs: She is alive… Hooray!!

Narrator: Snow White looked at the prince and fell in love.

Handsome Prince: Snow White, will you marry me?

Snow White: Of course, yes!

Narrator: Snow White and the handsome prince got married, and everyone lived happily ever after. Well, nearly everyone… *(Wicked Queen is seen in the background breaking the mirror in anger.)*

The Cat and the Mouse

Characters: Storyteller 1, Storyteller 2, Mouse, Cat

Storyteller 1: Here is the tale of a wily cat and a very foolish mouse who lived in a church

Mouse: I live in a mouse hole under the church pulpit.

Cat: Meow, I live in a cushion in the vestry.

Storyteller 2: One day, the cat knocked on the mouse hole door.

Cat: Knock, knock.

Mouse: Yes, Cat, how can I help you?

Cat: Mouse, I was thinking that since you and I both live alone, we should live together in the bell tower.

Mouse: Well, I'm not too fond of cats, but you have a nice smile, so why not?

Cat: We must store some food for winter, or else we shall be hungry.

Mouse: Why don't we put together our savings and buy a pot of fat?

Cat: What a clever idea. Where shall we hide it?

Cat: I know, let's hide it underneath the altar.

Storyteller 1: The cat placed the pot of fat underneath the altar. The cat and mouse went about their business until one day the cat said....

Cat: Little Mouse, my cousin just had a little kitten. She asked me to be the godmother. I must go to the christening. Will you be alright by yourself for the day?

Mouse: Of course I will. Go and enjoy yourself.

Storyteller 2: However, that was a lie. The cat went straight to the altar and opened the pot of fat.

Storyteller 1: The cat ate the top of the pot of fat. She went to the roof of the church, stretched out and licked her lips. When it got dark, she strolled home to the bell tower, happy and content.

Mouse: Did you have a good time at the christening?

Cat: It was very enjoyable.

Mouse: What is the kitten's name?

Cat: They called her ... Top Off.

Mouse: Top Off ... what a strange name.

Storyteller 1: A few days passed.

Cat: I have a craving for more fat. I have an idea. Mouse, you are not going to believe this, but another cousin of mine wants me to be the godmother of her baby kitten. Would you mind if I went to another christening?

Mouse: You do have a lot of family but go and enjoy yourself.

Storyteller 2: However, that was a lie. The cat went straight to the altar and opened the pot of fat.

Storyteller 1: The cat ate half the pot of fat. She went to the roof of the church, stretched out and licked her lips. When it got dark, she strolled home to the bell tower, happy and content.

Mouse: Did you have a good time at the christening?

Cat: It was very enjoyable.

Mouse: What is the kitten's name?

Cat: They called her ... Half-Empty

Mouse: Half Empty ... what a strange name.

Storyteller 1: A few days passed.

Cat: I have a craving for more fat. I have an idea. Mouse, you are not going to believe this, but another cousin of mine wants me to be the godmother of her baby kitten. Would you mind if I went to another christening?

Mouse: You do have a lot of family but go and enjoy yourself.

Storyteller 2: However, that was a lie. The cat went straight to the altar and opened the pot of fat.

Storyteller 1: The cat ate the bottom of the pot of fat. She went to the roof of the church, stretched out and licked her lips. When it got dark, she strolled home to the bell tower, happy and content.

Mouse: Did you have a good time at the christening?

Cat: It was very enjoyable.

Mouse: What is the kitten's name?

Cat: They called her ... All Gone.

Mouse: All Gone ... what very strange the cats give their kittens.

Storyteller 1: Winter came.

Mouse: Cat, I think we should get our pot of fat. I'm looking forward to it.

(She goes to the altar. The cat follows.)

Mouse: It's empty. There were never any christenings. Top Off, Half Empty, All Gone ... I'm a foolish mouse.

Cat: Mouse, don't take it personally. I'm always hungry and now I'm going to eat you up.

Storyteller 2: The mouse was too quick. She ran back to her safe mouse hole.

Mouse: I will never trust cats again.

The Frog Prince

Charaters: Storyteller 1, Storyteller 2, King, Princess, Frog/Prince,

Storyteller 1: Once upon a time there lived a beautiful princess.

Storyteller 2: She was very vain and selfish.

Princess: I'm so beautiful. I can't wear this dress. I need a new one. It's my birthday today. I wonder what my father. The king got me.

King: Happy Birthday Princess. I've got a wonderful present for you.

(She opens the present)

Princess: It's a ball.

King: Not just any old ball. It is a ball made out of gold. I got it specially made for you. There isn't another ball like it in the world.

Princess: I've never seen anything so beautiful in my life. A beautiful ball for a beautiful princess. I shall play with it in the garden.

Storyteller 1: She played with the ball every day.

Princess: If only I had a friend to play with. It is no fun playing ball by myself.

Frog: I'll play with you.

Princess: You, don't make me laugh. You are hideous. I'm not that desperate.

Frog: Your loss, I may look hideous, but I'm great fun to play with.

Storyteller 2: The princess flounced off, and the frog jumped back into the pond.

Storyteller 1: One day, the princess was playing with her ball by the pond.

Storyteller 2: She slipped on a stone. She wobbled, and then she wibbled, and she slipped into the pond.

Princess: Wait, where is my ball gone? I can't lose my ball. I can't lose my ball, it's my only friend.

Storyteller 1: She began looking for her ball. She couldn't find it and began to cry.

Princess: What shall I do. I've lost my beautiful golden ball.

(The frog appeared from the pond. He looks concerned and put his arm around the princess to try and comfort her.)

Frog: Why are you crying, princess?

Princess: I fell into the pond and lost my beautiful golden ball.

Frog: Don't cry. I'll help you find your golden ball.

Storyteller 1: The frog jumped back into the pond, and he found the golden ball.

Frog: You have to promise me something in return.

Princess: Anything I just want my ball back.

Frog: You must promise to be my friend.

Princess: I'll be your friend just give me back my ball.

Frog: Not so fast. You must promise to allow me to eat with you every night and sleep next to you every night.

Princess: I promise.

Frog: Here it is.

Princess: I got my ball back.

Storyteller 1: She ran towards the castle.

Frog: Princess, come back. You promised to be my friend. Wait for me.

Princess: In your dreams, I could never be friends with an ugly thing like you. Never bother me again.

Storyteller 2: That night, the princess and the king were eating their dinner.

Frog: Knock, knock. *(The frog knocks on the door.)*

King: Who is it? *(The frog hops in and bows before the king.)*

Frog: Ribbit, ribbit. Your majesty. I helped the princess to find her golden ball. She promised that she would be my friend and that I could eat with her at the table and sleep next to her.

Princess: I lied. I just wanted my ball back.

King: Princesses never break their promises. Welcome, come and have a seat and be our guest.

Storyteller 1: They ate their dinner.

Frog: That was delicious, now it's time for bed.

Princess: Seriously, you don't think you are coming anywhere near my bed.

King: You promised that he could sleep next to you. Remember princesses don't break their promises.

Storyteller 2: The princess picked up the frog by his neck and plonked him down in the corner of her bedroom.

Frog: Princess, I want to sleep in your bed.

Princess: You are disgusting. How can I sleep with you, Go away and never come back.

Storyteller 1: She threw the frog on the ground,

Frog: Splat!

Princess: Oh dear, I've killed him. What have I done? Oh, frog, please wake up. I'm so sorry. I'll be your friend. You can eat at my table and sleep next to me. Please, don't die. You are my only friend. (*She bends over and kisses him.*)

Storyteller 2: Suddenly, the frog turns into a handsome prince.

Frog/Prince: Thank you, princess, for breaking the spell.

Princess: What spell?

Frog/Prince: An evil witch turned me into a frog. She said only the friendship of a beautiful princess would break the spell.

Princess: I was so horrible to you. Can you forgive me?

Frog: Of course, I forgive you. Just promise you will never judge people by their appearance again.

Princess: I promise.

Storyteller 1: The prince and princess lived happily ever after.

Little Red Riding Hood

Characters: Three storytellers. Red Riding Hood, wolf, grandma, Red Riding Hood's mother, woodcutter, trees.

Storyteller 1: Once upon a time there lived a little girl called Little Red Riding Hood.

Storyteller 2: She was called Red Riding Hood because she always wore a cape with a red hood.

Storyteller 3: She was a very helpful little girl. One day her mother said...

Mother: Your grandmother is very ill. Take this basket of food and visit her. She would love to see you.

Red Riding Hood: Thank you, Mother. *(She takes the basket and off she goes to see her grandmother.)*

(Trees are scattered all over the stage.)

Tree 1: Look, there is a little girl walking in the forest by herself.

Tree 2: Do you think we should tell her it is dangerous?

Tree 3: She should know the Big Bad Wolf is always sniffing around.

Tree 1: The Big Bad Wolf is very nasty.

Tree 2: And scary.

Tree 3: He will eat anything.

Tree 1: I think we should tell her.

Tree 2: It is too late.

Tree 3: Here comes the Big Bad Wolf. *(Big Bad wolf enters.)*

Wolf: Hello, Red Riding Hood. Where are you off to on this lovely, fine day?

Red Riding Hood: I'm going to visit my grandmother. She is very sick, and I am going to bring her some food and these lovely flowers.

Wolf: But you are going the long way. *(He points to the opposite direction.)* That way is shorter.

Red Riding Hood: Oh thank you, Mr Wolf. *(Off she goes in the wrong direction.)*

(Wolf laughs loudly and runs off stage in the opposite direction.)

Tree 1: He told Red Riding Hood to go to her grandmother's house the long way.

Tree 2: He is up to something.

Tree 3: Something very bad.

(Grandmother comes on stage. She is sitting in a chair. She looks very sick. The wolf arrives.)

Wolf: Knock, knock.

Grandmother: Who is it?

Wolf: Red Riding Hood.

Grandmother: Come in, my dear. *(Wolf walks in and grandmother gets a fright.)*

Grandmother: You are not Red Riding Hood. *(She jumps up and starts to run around the room. The wolf chases her. Then there is a knock on the door. The wolf grabs the grandmother and puts her in the closet. He puts on her hat and glasses and gets into the chair.)*

Red Riding Hood: Knock, knock.

Wolf: Come in, Red Riding Hood.

Red Riding Hood: I've brought some nice food to help you get better.

Wolf: Why thank you, my dear.

Red Riding Hood: *(looks at grandmother)* Why grandmother, what big eyes you have!

Wolf: All the better to see you with, my dear.

Red Riding Hood: Why grandmother, what big ears you have!

Wolf: All the better to hear you with, my dear.

Red Riding Hood: Why grandmother, what big teeth you have!

Wolf: All the better to eat you with, my dear.

(The wolf jumps up and runs after Red Riding Hood. He chases her around the room.)

Tree 1: Do you hear screams?

Tree 2: We should call the woodsman to help.

Tree 3: Let's all shout for help together.

Trees: Woodsman, help, help!

(Woodsman comes racing in.)

Woodsman: What is all the noise about?

Tree 1: The Big Bad Wolf is in the grandmother's house.

Tree 2: He is chasing Red Riding Hood. He wants to eat her.

Tree 3: You need to save her.

(Woodsman runs into the house and grabs the wolf.)

Woodsman: What do you think you are doing? *(He waves the axe at him and chases him out of the house and off the stage.)*

Wolf: *(screams)* AARRGHHHHH!

Woodsman: And don't come back ever.

(Red Riding Hood gets her grandmother from the closet. They hug.)

Grandmother/Red Riding Hood: Thank you, Woodsman.

Grandmother: Would you like to stay for tea?

Woodsman: Oh yes, please.

Storyteller 1: They all sat down and enjoyed their tea.

Storyteller 2: The lesson of the story is...

Storyteller 3: Don't talk to strangers.

The Pied Piper of Hamelin

Characters: Two narrators, mayor, town crier, two town councillors, four rats, four townspeople, four children, a shopkeeper and two soldiers.

Narrator 1: Once upon a time in a town in Germany called Hamelin...

Narrator 2: They had a big rat problem. One day, the mayor called a town meeting.

Townsperson 1: Our home is full of rats.

Townsperson 2: The town councillors should do something before this causes a plague.

Townsperson 3: There are more and more of them every day.

Shopkeeper: They have eaten all my supplies.

Townsperson 4: They have bitten my baby. *(Rats come scurrying onto the stage and scare the mayor and townspeople.)*

Rats: *(Sing)* Rats, rats, rats. We fought the dogs and killed the cats, and bit the babies in the cradles, and ate the cheeses out of the vats, and licked the soup from the cooks' own ladles. Rats, rats, rats!

Mayor: I need to call the town councillors.

Town Crier: Hear ye! Hear ye! The meeting of the town councillors has commenced.

Town Councillor 1: We have to do something.

Town Councillor 2: We could set traps.

Town Councillor 1: They won't work; there are too many rats.

Town Councillor 2: I know! We could offer a reward to whoever can get rid of them.

Mayor: What a splendid idea. We could offer a thousand gold coins.

Town Crier: Hear ye! Hear ye! The mayor and the town councillors have offered a reward of a thousand gold coins to anyone who can get rid of the rats. (*He puts up some reward posters around the stage. Pied Piper enters and sees the posters and goes to see the mayor.*)

Pied Piper: I can get rid of the rats.

Mayor: You! But you are only a poor pied piper. How can YOU get rid of the rats?

Narrator 1: The pied piper began to play the most beautiful music. All the townspeople came to watch.

Rat 1: What beautiful music!

Rat 2: Where is it coming from?

Rat 3: Over there!

Rat 4: Let's follow it.

(*All the rats follow the musician.*)

Narrator 2: All the rats left the town and followed the pied piper. He walked into the river, and all the rats followed him.

(*All the rats are dragged downstream. They swim off the stage. Pied Piper comes out of the river and puts on his shoes. He goes to the mayor's office and knocks on his door.*)

Town Crier: May I help you?

Pied Piper: I demand to see the mayor. (*Mayor comes to the door.*)

Mayor: I don't have the gold coins. Besides, the rats are gone and are not coming back, so I'm not going to give you the money.

(All the townspeople come on stage and surround the mayor.)

Townspeople: Three cheers for the mayor. The rats are gone.

Mayor: Oh thank you, thank you so much. It was my pleasure.

Pied Piper: *(Gets angry)* But you didn't do anything! I got rid of the rats.

Mayor: *(Pushes him away)* All you did was play some music. Be off with you.

Pied Piper: Pay me, or you will rue the day that you crossed me. My revenge will destroy this town.

Mayor: Be off with you. Soldiers take him away.

(Soldiers escort him out of the town. Outside the town, children are playing. The pied piper plays his music.)

Pied Piper: Come with me, children.

Child 1: We love your music.

Child 2: Please keep playing.

Child 3: Let's follow the beautiful music.

Child 4: *(Falls over and picks himself up.)* Wait for me!

(Back in the town)

Townsperson 1: Mayor, please help us.

Shopkeeper: All the children have gone.

Mayor: This is the revenge of the pied piper.

Narrator 1: The children were never seen again. There were no longer any rats in Hamelin but there were also no longer any children.

Narrator 2: The moral of the story is always keep to your word.

Other Books by the Author:

Drama Start Series:

Drama Start: Drama Activities, Plays and Monologues for Children (Ages 3-8).

Drama Start Two: Drama Activities for Children (Ages 9-12).

Stage Start: 20 Plays for Children (Ages 3-12).

Movement Start: Over 100 Movement Activities and Stories for Children.

ESL Drama Start: Drama Activities and Plays for ESL Learners.

On Stage Series:

Aesop's Fables on Stage: A Collection of Plays Based on Aesop's Fables.

Fairy Tales on Stage: A Collection of Plays for Children.

Classics on Stage: A Collection of Plays Based on Classic Children's Stories.

Christmas Stories on Stage: A Collection of Plays for Children.

Panchatantra on Stage: A Collection of Plays for Children.

Hans Christian Andersen's Stories on Stage: A Collection of Plays for Children.

Oscar Wilde's Stories on Stage: A Collection of Plays based on Oscar Wilde's Short Stories.

Just So Stories on Stage: A Collection of Plays based on Rudyard Kipling's Just So Stories.

Animal Stories on Stage: A Collection of Plays based on Animal Stories.

More Fairy Tales on Stage: A Collection of Plays based on Fairy Tales.

Irish Legends on Stage: A Collection of Plays based on Irish Legends.

Bible Stories on Stage: A Collection of Plays based on Bible Stories.

Buddha Stories on Stage: A Collection of Plays based on Buddha Stories.

www.ingramcontent.com/pod-product-compliance
Lightning Source LLC
Chambersburg PA
CBHW021200080526
44588CB00008B/426